OCT 0 6

DATE DUE

GAYLORD			PRINTED IN U.S.A.

Marine Habitats
Life in Saltwater

Marine Habitats
Life in Saltwater

Salvatore Tocci

Franklin Watts
A Division of Scholastic Inc.
New York • Toronto • London • Auckland • Sydney
Mexico City • New Delhi • Hong Kong
Danbury, Connecticut

*For Thomas, who will sail one day beyond coastal waters
into the open ocean.*

Note to readers: Definitions for words in **bold** can be found in the Glossary at the back of this book.

Photographs ©: 2004: Corbis Images/Gavriel Jecan: 33 top; Dembinsky Photo Assoc.: 20 (Mary Liz Austin), 10 (Willard Clay), 27 bottom (Adam Jones), 27 top, 29 (Marilyn Kazmers), 38 (Bill Lea), 5 bottom, 30, 31 (Patti McConville), 43 (Gerhard Schulz), 22 (Mark J. Thomas); Hulton l Archive/Getty Images: 6; Monterey Bay Aquarium Research Institute/Kim Reisenbichler: 16 top; National Oceanic and Atmospheric Administration: 13, 14; Photo Researchers, NY: 45 (John Bova), 41 (Valerie Giles), 53 (Francois Gohier), 2 (David Hall), 37 (Stephen J. Krasemann), 33 bottom (Bud Lehnhausen), 26, 28, 35 top, 35 bottom, 51 (Andrew J. Martinez), 5 top, 46, 47 (Kenneth Murray), cover (Carl Purcell), 24 (Jeff Rotman), 49, 50 (Nancy Sefton), 23 (Vanessa Vick), 18 (Kent Wood); Seapics.com: 19 (Richard Ellis), 17 (Gregory Ochoki), 16 bottom (Doc White).

The photograph on the cover shows the ocean. The photograph opposite the cover page shows a marine habitat.

Library of Congress Cataloging-in-Publication Data

Tocci, Salvatore.
    Marine habitats : life in saltwater/ Salvatore Tocci.
        v. cm. — (Watts library)
    Includes bibliographical references (p.).
    Contents: The ocean — Coastal waters — Estuaries — Salt marshes — Swamps.
    ISBN 0-531-12306-5 (lib.bdg.)   0-531-16670-8 (pbk.)
    1. Marine ecology—Juvenile literature. 2. Brackish water ecology — Juvenile literature. [1. Marine ecology. 2. Ecology. 3. Ocean.] I. Title. II. Series.
QH541.5.S3T63 2003
577.7—dc22

2003016563

Contents

The pressure on the Trieste when it was on the bottom of the Marianas Trench was estimated to be 100,000 tons.

Deep Down

Jacques Piccard could not believe his eyes. He saw a fish that looked like a flounder. Soon after Piccard spotted it, the fish swam away and disappeared. He was shocked to have seen a fish because Piccard was on the ocean bottom, almost 7 miles (11 kilometers) below the surface. No one thought that anything could live that deep down.

On January 23, 1960, Piccard and Don Walsh took a United States Navy vessel named *Trieste* to the deepest spot on Earth's surface. This spot is the Marianas Trench in the Pacific Ocean, just

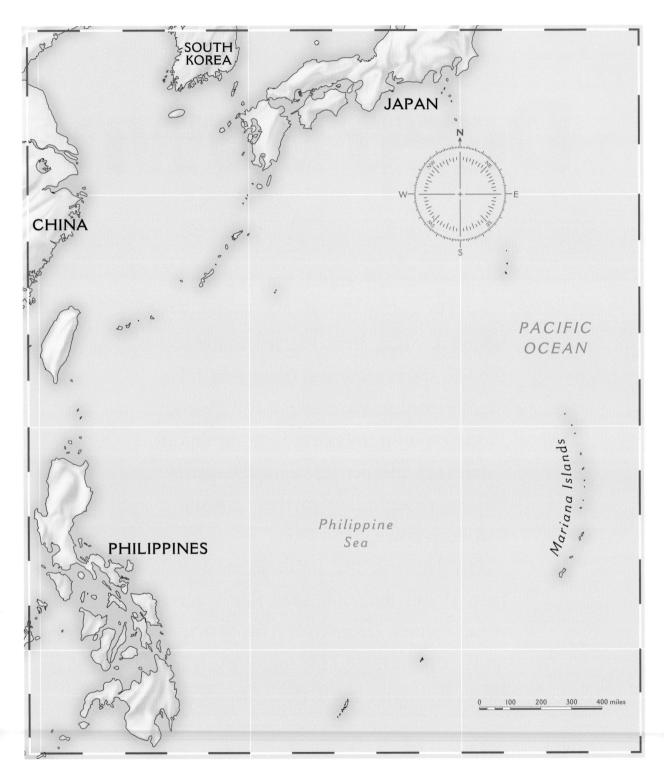

SOUTH
KOREA

JAPAN

N

NW NE

W E

SW SE

S

CHINA

PACIFIC
OCEAN

Mariana Islands

Philippine
Sea

PHILIPPINES

0   100   200   300   400 miles

east of the Philippine Islands. To appreciate how deep this spot is, imagine that Mount Everest, which is the highest point on Earth, rose from the bottom of the Marianas Trench. There still would be 1 mile (1.6 km) of water above the top of Mount Everest!

The *Trieste* looks like a submarine, but it is actually a bathyscaphe. The word *bathyscaphe* comes from two Greek words that mean "deep boat." A bathyscaphe is built to travel deep underwater, where the pressure pushing against the outside of the vessel is tremendous. The *Trieste* was 35,810 feet (11 km) deep in the Marianas Trench, where the pressure on the hull was more than one thousand times greater than it was at sea level.

In the more than forty years since Piccard and Walsh set the record for the world's deepest dive, no one has even come close to breaking it. These two men are still the only humans who have ever visited the deepest part of the ocean, which is just one of the world's marine, or saltwater, habitats.

Long Voyage

The trip from the ocean surface to the Marianas Trench and back took almost nine hours. However, the *Trieste* spent only about twenty minutes at the bottom.

The Marianas Trench, which lies to the east of the Philippine Islands, is sometimes called the "Grand Canyon of the Pacific."

The oceanic zone makes up about 90 percent of the ocean's area.

Chapter One

The Ocean

A **habitat** is the place in which an **organism**, or living thing, lives. The ocean is the world's largest marine habitat. It covers about 70 percent of Earth's surface. Scientists divide the ocean into two areas, or zones. One is the **benthic zone**, which is the ocean bottom. All the water above the ocean bottom makes up the **pelagic zone**. Scientists further divide the pelagic zone into smaller zones, depending on how far they are from land.

The deep water of the open ocean is called the **oceanic zone**. This zone is found beyond the continental shelf, which is a shallow landmass that extends an average of 40 miles (65 km) from every continent. At some point, the continental shelf drops off sharply. This is where the oceanic zone begins.

Like the land surface of Earth, the ocean bottom is very uneven. Mountain ranges and deep trenches, such as the Marianas Trench, are found scattered throughout the ocean floor. In 1977, another bathyscaphe named *Alvin* descended into one of these trenches near the Galapagos Islands off the coast of Ecuador. When *Alvin* reached a depth of 1.5 miles (2.4 km), the scientists aboard observed what looked like black smoke billowing out of the ocean floor, or benthic zone.

Extremely Hot

The water coming from a volcanic vent can reach 750° Fahrenheit (400° Celsius), which is four times hotter than the boiling point of water.

The Benthic Zone

Sometimes cold ocean water seeps down through cracks in the sea bottom. This water eventually reaches the hot, melted rock called magma deep inside Earth. There, the water is heated to temperatures far above boiling. However, the high pressure at such depths keeps the water from boiling. The superheated water, mixed with the minerals from dissolved rocks, rushes out of vents, or holes in the ocean floor, like lava that erupts from a volcano. The scientists aboard the *Alvin* had discovered a deep-sea volcanic vent.

Even more surprising to the scientists aboard *Alvin* was another observation they made. They did not expect to find many living things this far down in the ocean. However, they did. They saw organisms in a variety of shapes and sizes. Many were moving about, either swimming or crawling along the

seafloor. These creatures included fish, shrimp, crabs, clams, mussels, and worms. Some of the shrimp were bright red and had no eyes. The clams were almost 1 foot (25 centimeters) in length. Another animal was orange and looked like a dandelion.

Perhaps the strangest-looking organisms were the giant tube worms. These organisms are thin and long, reaching a length of more than 6 feet (2 meters). Giant tube worms grow at a rate of more than 30 inches (75 cm) a year, making them the fastest-growing marine organism known. Their white bodies are crowned with reddish tops. They have no eyes or

Can you see why volcanic vents are also called "black smokers"?

Giant tube worms have been found only near volcanic vents in the Pacific Ocean.

mouths, and they do not eat. Rather, they get the food they need from other organisms called bacteria that live inside the worms.

Bacteria are the most common organisms living near volcanic vents. There can be so many bacteria that they look like a blinding snowstorm moving deep in the oceanic zone or a thick carpet covering the benthic zone. These bacteria make food, just as plants do on land.

Plants use sunlight to make food. The bacteria, however, are too deep in the ocean to get any sunlight. Rather, they use a chemical that is highly concentrated in the water and comes from volcanic vents. This is hydrogen sulfide, which smells like rotten eggs. The bacteria change the hydrogen sulfide into food. The bacteria living inside giant tube worms make more food than they need. The giant tube worms depend on this excess food to survive. In turn, shrimps and crabs that live near a volcanic vent feed on the tube worms.

The Oceanic Zone

In the oceanic zone, life on or very near the sea bottom exists almost entirely near volcanic vents. Organisms living closer to the surface but still below 3,500 feet (1,000 m) are more plentiful and widespread. However, even these organisms have rarely been observed in their natural habitat by humans. Most of what scientists know about them comes from studies of dead organisms that float to the surface.

Scientists have discovered some interesting **adaptations**, or ways in which these organisms survive the harsh conditions of the deep ocean. Such adaptations can be seen in the vampire squid, which has been observed at depths of more than 15,000 feet (4,500 m). This animal gets its name from when it was first seen, because it was described as being as black as night with white jaws and bloodred eyes.

Compared to its total body size, the vampire squid has the largest eyes of any animal in the world. With a body size of only 6 inches (15 cm), each eye measures 1 inch (2.5 cm) across, or about the size of an eye of a full-grown dog. The

Despite its name, the vampire squid is a docile animal.

The gulper eel is adapted to eating a large meal all at once because food is hard to find in the deep ocean.

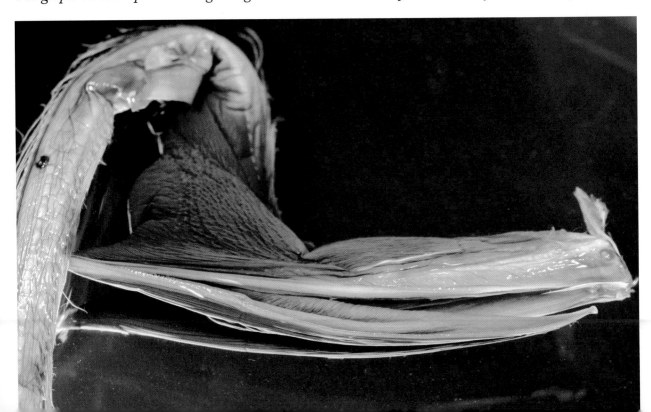

squid's giant eyes help locate whatever food might come its way in the darkness of the oceanic zone.

Another organism found in the deep ocean is the gulper or umbrellamouth eel. This fish's body is nothing more than a mouth and a very long stomach. It feeds by opening its mouth very wide to capture as many shrimp and tiny fish as it can.

Closer to the Surface

Many more types of organisms are found in the oceanic zone in waters that are less than 3,500 feet (1,000 m) from the surface. Many of the organisms living in this habitat are as strange looking as those living in deeper waters. The viper fish is one example. With its sharp, fanglike teeth, this fish looks like a terrifying monster. However, the viper fish is only a few inches long. Some viper fish have black bodies that blend in with the darkness. Others are color-less and are very difficult to spot. Their body colors protect viper fish from **predators** searching for organisms to eat. The organisms that are eaten by other organisms are known as **prey**.

The waters of the oceanic zone that are within 330 feet (100 m) of the surface are the most heavily populated. Sunlight can penetrate the water at these depths. As a result, tiny organisms can use the

The teeth of a viper fish are so big that it may not be able to close its mouth.

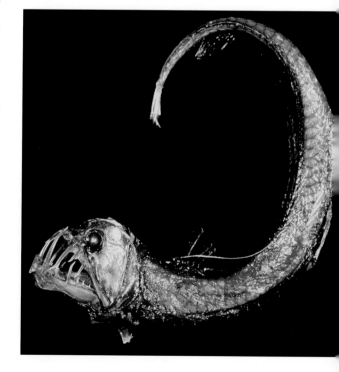

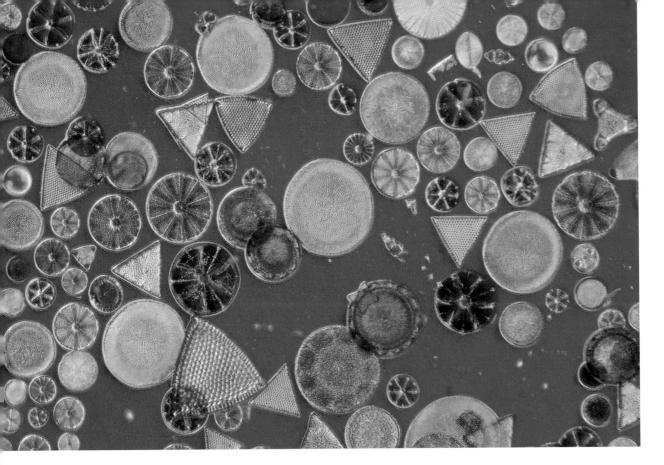

The most common phytoplankton in the oceanic zone are called diatoms, which have beautiful colors and complex shapes.

sunlight to make food through a process called **photosynthesis**. These organisms are known as **phytoplankton**.

In addition to sunlight, phytoplankton need certain substances, such as water, to perform photosynthesis. Obviously,

Blue Waters

Although sunlight appears white, it actually consists of all the colors that can be seen in a rainbow. However, the red, orange, and yellow colors do not penetrate very far into water. In contrast, the green, blue, and violet colors penetrate much deeper and give ocean water its dark, blue-green color. Generally, no sunlight penetrates ocean water below 490 feet. At these depths, there is only darkness, except for light given off by some deep-sea organisms.

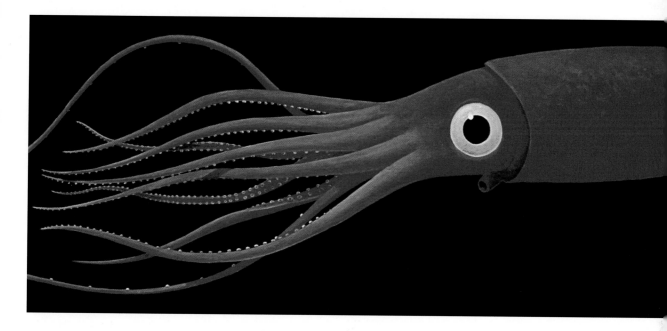

water is plentiful in the ocean. Light, on the other hand, can be very limited. Therefore, the food produced per square mile of ocean is very low. However, the ocean covers such a vast portion of Earth that the oceanic zone is a major site of photosynthesis. About half of the photosynthesis that occurs on Earth takes place in the oceanic zone.

All this photosynthesis produces enough food to support a variety of life that exists near the surface of the oceanic zone. Life near the surface includes such organisms as sharks, manta rays, marlins, squid, whales, dolphins, otters, and sea lions. All these creatures make the oceanic zone their habitat. Many of them even venture closer to shore.

This organism, known as the giant squid, is the largest animal without a backbone in the world. It can reach 60 feet (18 m) in length and can weigh almost 1 ton.

*The neritic zone lies above
the continental shelf.*

Chapter Two

Coastal Waters

Many organisms from the open ocean often venture into waters that are close to land. These coastal waters are divided into two zones. One is the **neritic zone**, which consists of the ocean water that covers the continental shelf. The neritic zone is the habitat for more organisms than any other area of the ocean.

Living things are much more common in the neritic zone because this area of the ocean contains many more nutrients than the water in the oceanic zone.

Coral reefs are home to many kinds of colorful fish.

A **nutrient** is a substance that an organism needs to live and grow. Nutrients are carried into the neritic zone by water that runs off the land. Strong ocean currents also bring nutrients to the neritic zone from the ocean bottom.

With all these nutrients, the neritic zone is rich with phytoplankton. More food is made by the phytoplankton in 1 square mile (2.6 sq km) of the neritic zone than in 1 square mile of any other zone of the ocean. All this food can support abundant and diverse life-forms. Nowhere is this more obvious than in a **coral reef**.

Coral Reefs

A coral reef is a ridge of rocky material that has been made by marine organisms in the neritic zones of tropical areas. In fact, coral reefs are the largest structures made by living things. Coral reefs are places brimming with organisms that have striking colors, strange shapes, and fascinating habits. Nowhere else in the seas can you find so many different organisms living so closely together. More than 100,000 kinds of plants and animals that live on coral reefs have been identified and described. Scientists estimate that between 500,000 and 2,000,000 kinds of organisms may actually inhabit coral reefs. No other marine habitat has the diversity of life, or **biodiversity**, as is found in coral reefs.

Neritic zones outside the tropics are also habitats for a wide variety of marine organisms, although not nearly as many as those found in a coral reef. Animals that live in the neritic zone

Very Long

The Great Barrier Reef in Australia spans a distance equal in length to the eastern coast of the United States.

Commercial fishing boats are a common sight in the neritic zone.

Kelp beds can grow so tall and thick in the neritic zone that they are called underwater forests.

include squids, walruses, seals, sea turtles, and sea snakes. Fishes, however, are the dominant group.

Animals are not the only organisms that live in neritic zones. Plantlike organisms known as **algae** also live there. One example is a kind of seaweed called kelp. Algae are similar to plants in that they carry out photosynthesis. They differ from plants in that they do not have roots, stems, or true leaves.

Different kinds of kelp thrive in cold salt water. Some types can grow at a rate of 20 inches (50 cm) per day and can reach a length of hundreds of feet. Kelp often forms large bunches, or beds, that are firmly attached to the sea bottom. These beds provide food and protection for many types of organisms living in neritic zones.

A Common Problem

Most marine animals face the same problem. They live in a habitat in which the water contains about 3 percent salt. This is higher than the percentage of salt inside these organisms. Most of this salt is a chemical called sodium chloride, which is present in table salt.

The lower percentage of salt inside these organisms means that they have a higher percentage of water in their bodies than the ocean does. As a result, these organisms tend to lose water from their bodies. Even though they live in water, these marine animals must avoid becoming dehydrated. To keep as much water in their bodies as possible, these organisms drink a lot of water. Various body parts, such as the gills of fish, pump out the salt that is in this water. These animals also do not produce much urine, which is a way they save water.

The Intertidal Zone

The ocean waters closest to shore make up the **intertidal zone**. The abundance and variety of life within this zone depends on the tide. The tide divides an intertidal zone into four smaller zones. These are the low tide, middle tide, high tide, and spray zones.

The low tide zone is farthest from land and is always underwater, unless the tide is unusually low. With plenty of water, nutrients, and sunlight, the low tide zone is the most populated of all the intertidal zones.

Animals that live in the low tide zone include sea stars, sea

World Record

The difference between the point on land that ocean water reaches at low tide compared to the point it reaches at high tide is called the tidal range. The average tidal range for ocean waters throughout the world is about 3 feet (1 m). However, the Bay of Fundy in Canada holds the world record, with a tidal range of slightly more than 50 feet (15 m).

A sea star uses tiny feet called suction tubes to slide across the sea floor. Hundreds of these suction tubes are located on the bottom of each arm.

urchins, and sea anemones. Sea stars exist in a variety of shapes and colors. All sea stars, however, have arms that extend out from their bodies in the center. This gives them a starlike appearance. As long as a sea star keeps part of its main body, it can regenerate any arm it loses.

The sea urchin is called the pincushion of the sea because of the spines that cover its body. These animals are well adapted to their marine habitat. Their spines protect them from predators. Their five strong teeth scrape algae from rocks and the sea bottom. Sea anemones belong to a group of animals whose name means "flower animals." They got this name because of their many tentacles that wave in the water and make these animals look like flowers. Sea anemones can easily attach themselves to rocks from which they use their tentacles to catch plankton and small fish.

The middle tide zone is closer to land. This zone is covered

Sea urchins come in a variety of colors, especially in shades of purple. A sea urchin's mouth is located on the underside of its body.

and uncovered with water from the tides twice a day. Animals with shells are the most common organisms that live in this zone. These include barnacles, crabs, mussels, clams, and snails. When the water is at high tide, most of the animals in this zone move about, searching for food.

The high tide zone is the next area closer to land. As its

Sea anemones spend most of their lives in one place, usually attached to rocks on the seafloor. They use tiny poison darts attached to their tentacles to capture prey.

Mussels have also been seen near deep-sea vents.

Mussel Threads

The threads from mussels were once woven into cloth to make it more resistant to tearing.

name suggests, this zone is covered with water only during high tide. Again, animals with shells are the most common organisms living in this marine habitat.

Although the middle tide and high tide zones are rich in nutrients and receive plenty of sunlight, they pose a challenge for the organisms living in them. As the tide goes out, the organisms become exposed to the air. Exposure to the air can cause a marine organism to lose water. If an organism loses too much water, it dies.

To reduce the loss of water, organisms with shells, such as clams and mussels, keep their shells tightly closed. Snails retreat into their shells. They also secrete a layer of mucus to cover the opening to seal in moisture.

Besides being exposed to the air, these organisms must also be able to withstand the force of pounding waves. Organisms with shells are protected from being crushed on the rocks. Those without shells bury themselves in the sea bottom or attach themselves to rocks. Some organisms have more than one adaptation. Mussels, for example, are protected by their shells. They also secrete fine threads to attach themselves to rocks.

The spray zone is closest to shore. This zone is rather dry and gets wet only during high tide and when the wind sprays water onto the land. With so little water available, very few plants grow in this area. Life in the spray zone is limited mostly to barnacles and other small animals with shells. Barnacles are known for their ability to cling to rocks, where they feed by filtering the water for tiny organisms known as **plankton**.

Most people believe that barnacles are related to mussels and clams because they have hard shells. However, barnacles are more closely related to crabs and shrimps.

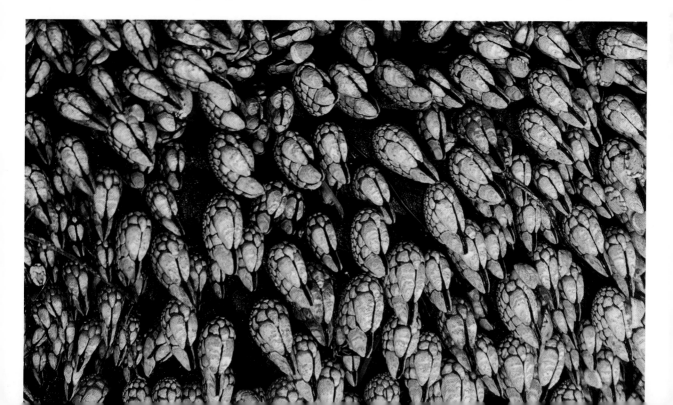

San Francisco Bay is an example of an estuary.

Chapter Three

Estuaries

Where ocean and land meet, the salt water of the ocean mixes with the freshwater flowing out of rivers and streams. This mixing of salt water and freshwater produces a partially enclosed body of water known as an **estuary**. Estuaries exist in many shapes and sizes and go by different names. Glacier Bay, Puget Sound, Boston Harbor, Cook Inlet, and Indian River Lagoon are all examples of estuaries.

However, not all bays, sounds, harbors, inlets, and lagoons are estuaries. Two conditions must be met for a body of water to be called an estuary. First, the water must be a mixture of salt water and freshwater. Second, the freshwater must be partially blocked by a landmass so that it does not flow directly into the ocean. The landmass protects the water in an estuary from being subjected to the full force of ocean waves and winds. However, the water level in an estuary changes with the tides.

The mixing of salt water and freshwater creates a unique habitat for organisms. Estuaries receive nutrients from freshwater running off the land and from salt water flowing in from the ocean with the tide. With so many nutrients, estuaries are among the most productive habitats on Earth. More food is made by photosynthesis in 1 square mile (2.6 sq km) of an estuary than in 1 square mile (2.6 sq km) of a forest or farmland. As a result, the biodiversity in an estuary, such as a saltwater bay, is striking. Glacier Bay in Alaska is one example.

A Pacific Ocean Estuary

Located within Glacier Bay National Park and Preserve, Glacier Bay is an estuary formed by the waters of the Pacific Ocean mixing with freshwater rivers and streams that are fed by melting snow and ice. The bay contains large populations of intertidal organisms, including clams, mussels, shrimps, and crabs. Glacier Bay is also the habitat for nearly two hundred kinds of fish, including salmon, cod, and halibut.

The abundance of organisms found in Glacier Bay is a dining invitation for the marine predators that swim in from the Pacific Ocean. One such predator is the humpback whale.

Glacier Bay was covered by a huge ice sheet when the first visitors from Europe arrived in the area in the late 1700s.

The humpback whale got its name from the humped look of its back as it dives.

Each summer, fifteen to twenty humpback whales can be seen feeding in Glacier Bay. A humpback whale feeds by opening its mouth and taking in tons of water. The whale then expels this water back out through its mouth. On the way out, the water first passes through baleen plates, which are hard, bonelike structures that act like a strainer. The baleen plates are organized like the teeth in a comb. Hundreds of baleen plates are arranged in rows and hang from the whale's top jaw. After the water has been filtered, the whale uses its tongue to scrape the plankton that have been trapped on the baleen. A humpback whale eats about 1 ton (2,000 pounds) of food each day. As winter approaches, the humpback whales leave the Glacier Bay estuary and head for warmer waters. Most head for Hawaii, which is about 2,800 miles (4,500 km) away.

An Atlantic Ocean Estuary

An estuary that is formed in part by the Atlantic Ocean is Chesapeake Bay. In fact, Chesapeake Bay is the largest and most productive estuary in the United States. About 2,700 different kinds of plants and animals live in the bay. The blue crab is probably the most famous of all the marine organisms that make the Chesapeake Bay their home.

The blue crab is named for its two bright blue claws. The crab uses these claws to defend itself against predators and to obtain food. It feeds on a variety of organisms, including worms, small fish, clams, mussels, and even plants. In turn, blue crabs are eaten by catfish, striped bass, sea turtles, and

Their Habitat

Humpback whales are found in all the oceans of the world.

even other blue crabs. Blue crabs are more likely to be eaten when they are molting, or shedding their old shells and developing new ones. At this stage, their bodies do not have much protection.

Molting blue crabs usually seek protection among the eelgrass that thrives in Chesapeake Bay. In fact, many marine organisms in the bay hide in the eelgrass for protection. These organisms include bass, flounder, weakfish, bluefish,

The two foreign words that make up the scientific name of the blue crab mean "beautiful swimmer" and "tasty."

Like all grasses, eelgrass is a flowering plant.

and scallops. The eelgrass is not only a safe place to hide, it also helps to lessen the impact of wave action on the shore. In turn, this helps to reduce the erosion, or washing away, of the sand along the shore.

A Mystery

The San Francisco Bay estuary is the largest estuary on the lower west coast of North America. The estuary is home to eight million people and is the source of water for a large part of California. Like many estuaries, San Francisco Bay has been polluted with garbage, toxic chemicals, wastewater, and oil spills.

At the start of the 1990s, oil-covered birds began washing

An Unwelcome Guest

Some organisms living in Chesapeake Bay are not native to this habitat. One example is the mute swan. These animals were first brought to New York from Europe and Asia during the 1800s. From New York, they were introduced to other parts of the United States. The swans were sought after because of their beauty. Mostly, they were placed in gardens and zoos.

In the 1960s, five mute swans escaped from their cages in Maryland. They soon made Chesapeake Bay their home. In 1986, 264 mute swans were counted in the bay. In 1999, almost four thousand were counted. These swans became a threat to other organisms living in the bay because one swan can eat up to 8 pounds (3 kilograms) of eelgrass a day. These swans also destroy other birds' nests. Aware of how these swans are disrupting life in the Chesapeake Bay, scientists are trying to eliminate these unwelcome guests. One method involves covering their eggs with oil so that they do not hatch.

up on shore in San Francisco Bay. Over the years, their numbers increased. In 2001, more than one thousand seabirds came ashore covered with oil. Only half of them could be saved. Although the problem existed for more than ten years, the source of the oil remained a mystery.

To find out where the birds might have encountered the oil, scientists decided to study water currents and wind patterns. Their findings led them to an oil tanker that had sunk just outside San Francisco Bay in 1953. The oil was eventually removed from the sunken vessel so that it could no longer pollute the estuary.

Oil spills are a major threat to marine life, such as seabirds.

*A saltwater marsh is
often found on the
fringe of an estuary.*

Chapter Four

Salt Marshes

A **salt marsh** is a marine habitat in which plants that can tolerate salty conditions are the dominant organisms. A salt marsh forms when incoming tides deposit sediment across low-lying land. These sediments slowly accumulate and turn into mud flats. Saltwater plants then start to take root. These plants grow where the water is shallow and slow-moving. Over time, the death and decay of these plants produces a marine habitat that is rich in nutrients. The salt marsh can then support the growth of hundreds of different kinds of organisms.

In addition to being habitats for many organisms, salt marshes serve other important roles. These marine habitats act like giant sponges, soaking up large volumes of water. This water slowly seeps down into the ground. As a result, salt marshes help create groundwater, which is a source of drinking water for many communities. By soaking up all this water, these marshes also help prevent the flooding of surrounding areas.

Food Factories

Salt marshes are also among the most productive food factories on Earth. This marine habitat supports a large amount of vegetation, including both phytoplankton and plants. The main source of food in the habitat comes from the photosynthesis carried out by this vegetation. The vegetation in 1 acre (0.4 hectare) of salt marsh produces twice as much food as the crops planted on 1 acre (0.4 ha) of most farms.

Many plants that live in a salt marsh are called **halophytes**, which are salt-tolerant plants. The halophyte found closest to the water is cordgrass. Without cordgrass, a marsh is not likely to develop. This marsh plant has a hardy root system that holds together the muddy bottom. Cordgrass also serves as a major source of food for many marsh organisms. However, these organisms do not feed directly on the cordgrass. Rather, they feed on the **detritus**, or decaying matter, left by dead cordgrass plants. A salt marsh is rich in detritus.

Like estuaries, salt marshes are affected by ocean tides.

When the tide comes in, the marsh is replenished with ocean water that carries nutrients to the halophytes. When the tide goes out, the water transports detritus from the marsh out to the sea. This detritus provides nutrients for marine animals living in ocean waters.

Like marine animals living in the ocean, halophytes living in a marsh face the threat of dehydration. The salt concentration is higher in marsh water than it is in the plants. As a result, the water concentration is higher inside the plants than it is in the marsh. Because of this, water would normally flow from the halophytes into their surroundings. Salt, on the other hand, would move into the plants. The loss of water and the gain of salt would lead to dehydration and then death for the plants.

To conserve water and stay alive, halophytes concentrate salt in their roots. This makes the salt concentration higher in the roots than it is in the surrounding soil. At the same time, this makes the water concentration higher in the soil than it is in the roots. As a result, water flows into the roots and is then transported to the rest of the plant. Many of these plants also have glands that excrete salt. These adaptations to take in water and get rid of salt help cordgrass and other halophytes avoid dehydration.

Marsh Animals

A variety of animals make salt marshes their home. These organisms include small fish, snails, mussels, clams, crabs, oysters, turtles, snakes, and alligators. The American alligator usually lives in freshwater. However, these alligators also inhabit salt marshes throughout the Southeast.

These alligators eat just about anything they can find in a marsh, including fish, turtles, and snails. They hunt underwater and swallow their meals whole. With such big appetites,

An alligator may live thirty-five to fifty years and grow to be 18 feet (5.5 m) long.

An Endangered Animal

The American alligator was once threatened with extinction. An estimated ten million alligators were killed between 1870 and 1960. Most were killed for their hides, which were used to make shoes and handbags.

In 1967, the U.S. government listed the American alligator as an endangered animal. Killing alligators became illegal. By 1987, the alligator population had recovered. In fact, the population recovered so well that in 1996, Florida instituted programs to control their population. Today, the alligator is no longer listed as endangered.

the alligators help control the numbers of small animals that would otherwise devour the vegetation that holds the marshes together.

Alligators are valuable to salt marshes in another way. An alligator uses its mouth and claws to clear out a space among the vegetation. It then uses its body and powerful tail to create a depression in the mud. These "gator holes" stay full of water throughout the year, including the dry season. These holes serve as habitats for other marsh animals that would likely die without the water during the dry season.

A Perfect Habitat

At certain times of the year, the small pools of water scattered throughout a salt marsh are one of its most obvious features. These pools are formed by the rain, high tides, and runoff from the land. However, these areas are dry much of the time. Marsh areas that go through these regular cycles of flooding and drying make a perfect habitat for mosquitoes. Without this wet-dry cycle, mosquitoes cannot reproduce because the females will not lay eggs directly in water.

Aware of the diseases that mosquitoes can cause, people have long tried to eliminate them from salt marshes. Up through the late 1970s, marshes were drained and sprayed with pesticides. These methods killed adult mosquitoes, but they also destroyed much more. Draining the marshes removed the water that other organisms needed to survive. The pesticides also killed organisms besides the mosquitoes.

Today, the most common method used to control mosquitoes is known as **impounding**. This method involves building up the marsh to create a dike, or barrier, around an area in which mosquitoes breed. Water is then pumped into the impounded area so that it remains flooded. As a result, the mosquitoes cannot reproduce because there is no time of the year when the area is dry.

One square foot (930 sq cm) of water in a marsh may contain as many as ten thousand eggs.

Saltwater swamps such as this one are found in tropical areas throughout the world, including Africa, North and South America, and India.

Chapter Five

Swamps

Unlike the American alligator, the American crocodile prefers living in saltwater. These crocodiles can be found in both salt marshes and **swamps**. Unlike a salt marsh, a swamp is completely covered with water for most of the year. The water can be anywhere from several inches to a few feet deep. Saltwater swamps are formed when coastal waters flow into inland areas. Like estuaries and marshes, swamps are affected by the tides.

Like other marine habitats, a swamp causes organisms to lose water and accumulate salt. However, this problem is often more serious in a swamp than in other marine habitats. For example, the salt concentration in the water of some areas of a swamp can be up to three times higher than the concentration in ocean water.

This high salt concentration is the result of repeated flooding of a swamp with ocean water. After each flood, some of the water evaporates slowly. The salt, however, remains behind. Over time, the amount of salt in swamp water builds up. Besides losing water, another problem swamp organisms face is getting enough oxygen, because only low levels of oxygen exist in the mud. Most organisms need oxygen to obtain energy from the nutrients they consume. To survive in a swamp, organisms must have adaptations to keep them from losing too much water. They must also have adaptations to help them get enough oxygen.

Mangrove Trees

One organism that is well adapted to conditions in a swamp is the mangrove tree. In fact, mangrove trees thrive in swamps. They grow so well that these marine habitats are sometimes called mangrove swamps. Few other trees can survive the problems posed by the high salt concentrations and low oxygen levels that exist in swamps.

To prevent dehydration, some types of mangrove trees get rid of excess salt by secreting it out through their leaves. This salt accumulates as crystals on the leaves, where it eventually gets washed away by rain. Their leaves are also covered with a waxy substance that reduces the loss of water through evaporation.

To get more oxygen, the roots of mangrove trees have structures that look like shoots that stick out above the water and are covered with small holes that take in oxygen directly from the air.

The seeds of mangrove trees are also adapted to conditions in a swamp. Most seeds must be planted in soil before they can start to grow. However, the oxygen-poor mud in a swamp provides an unfavorable environment for seeds to start their growth. Unlike other seeds, mangrove seeds actually start to grow while they are still attached to the tree. Once they are large enough, the young plants detach themselves from the parent tree. The young plants are then carried away by the

If the seeds of a mangrove tree should fall into the water, they can float until they encounter land.

Cleaning the Waters

Among other important jobs, mangrove trees clean the water before it returns to the sea by filtering out the silt, or fine sediments.

slow-moving water. Upon encountering land, they can establish their roots in the mud, where they continue to grow. On average, a mangrove tree grows about 1 foot (30 cm) per year.

The Mangrove Community

An entire community of living things can be found both on and near mangrove trees. Mussels, clams, oysters, sea urchins, barnacles, and worms are some of the organisms that live on the roots of mangrove trees. These animals filter the water around them to feed on plankton.

The feather duster worm is one example of an animal with an interesting adaptation that allows it to filter swamp water. This worm lives in a tube about the length and width of a soda straw. When feeding, the worm sticks its head out of the end of the tube and uses its "feathers" to trap plankton. The tiny

Feather duster worms live in groups that attach to the roots of mangrove trees.

organisms are then brushed into the worm's mouth, which is located in the center of its "feathers."

Other swamp organisms live among the mangrove roots and move about to seek food. These include young fish, crabs, shrimp, and jellyfish. The upside-down jellyfish has an unusual habit when it is not moving through swamp water in search of food. Like all jellyfish, this animal moves through the water with its tentacles pointing downward. However, when resting on the muddy bottom, this jellyfish points its tentacles upward. This exposes the algae that live inside the jellyfish to sunlight. The algae depend on the sunlight for photosynthesis.

A variety of organisms can also be found living close to the mangrove trees above water. This includes a type of crab that is adapted for climbing trees. With its powerful claws, the crab climbs the tree to avoid the rising water from an incoming tide. While in the treetop, the crab takes the opportunity to eat the mangrove leaves.

The upside-down jellyfish has a brown and white body that camouflages it from predators.

Its Name

The feather duster worm gets its name because it looks like a cleaning device made of feathers.

The leaves and branches of mangrove trees serve as a habitat for many birds, including herons, egrets, warblers, and cuckoos. Some birds are so common to this marine habitat that the word *mangrove* has become part of their common name. The mangrove cuckoo is one example. This bird feeds on insects, which are the most abundant organisms in a mangrove community. Like salt marshes, swamps are full of mosquitoes.

Mangrove Fruit

The fruit of mangrove trees is also a source of food for some swamp animals, such as turtles.

A Sensitive Habitat

Mangrove trees are especially sensitive to oil spills. Any oil that gets into a swamp can cover the root openings that the trees use to get oxygen. As a result, the oil can suffocate and kill the trees. In September 2002, a cargo ship ran aground off the coast of South Africa. The ship was transporting more than 1,000 tons of fuel oil that quickly began to wash ashore. A retaining wall was built to prevent the oil from reaching the nearby mangrove swamps. These swamps are part of a marine park that is the habitat of the largest population of rhinoceroses in the world.

Another threat to mangrove swamps is the cutting down of trees. Mangrove swamps are often close to coral reefs. The trees are removed to make way for hotels, marinas, restaurants, and shops for the increasing number of tourists who wish to explore the biodiversity that exists on a coral reef. Many types of mangrove trees are also sought after as exotic woods used to make furniture.

Other mangrove trees are also cut down to make way for shrimp farms and rice paddies. These food-producing enterprises provide a source of income for the local communities. However, unexpected problems can arise, as happened in a mangrove swamp that spreads across the coastlines of India and Bangladesh. This is the only place in the world where the Bengal tiger has made its habitat in a mangrove swamp.

Over the years, the local people gradually cut down mangrove trees to make way for rice paddies. The destruction of the trees destroyed the habitat of many animals, including the swamp deer. At one time, these deer were a major source of food for Bengal tigers. Today, not a single deer can be found in the swamp. Without the deer, the Bengal tigers have been forced to search elsewhere for food. About one hundred people living near the rice paddies are killed each year by hungry Bengal tigers, which once had enough food to sustain them in their marine habitat.

The Bengal tiger has made its habitat in a mangrove swamp known as the Sundarbans in Asia.

Glossary

adaptation—feature that increases an organism's chance of survival

algae—plantlike organisms that carry out photosynthesis

benthic zone—ocean bottom

biodiversity—variety of life that is found in a particular area, such as a coral reef

coral reef—ridge of rocky material found in tropical seas

detritus—the decayed remains of dead organisms

estuary—partially enclosed body of water formed by the mixing of saltwater and freshwater

habitat—place in which an organism lives

halophyte—salt-tolerant plant

impounding—method use to control mosquito populations in marsh areas

intertidal zone—ocean water closest to the shore

neritic zone—ocean water that lies above the continental shelf

nutrient—substance an organism needs to live and grow

oceanic zone—deep water of the open sea beyond the continental shelf

organism—living thing

pelagic zone—open ocean

photosynthesis—process through which organisms use light to make food

phytoplankton—very tiny organisms that live in water and carry out photosynthesis

plankton—very tiny organisms that live in water

predator—organism that feeds on another organism

prey—organism that is eaten by another organism

salt marsh—open, wet area in which plants dominate the habitat

swamp—inland area that is completely covered by water most of the year

To Find Out More

Books

Blaxland, Beth. *Mangroves.* Water Worlds. Chelsea House Publications, 2001.

Fleisher, Paul. *Salt Marsh.* Webs of Life. Marshall Cavendish Corp., 1999.

Galko, Francine. *Sea Animals.* Animals in Their Habitats. Heinemann Library, 2002.

L'Hommedieu, Arthur John. *Ocean Tide Pool.* Habitats. Children's Press, 1998.

Noyed, Robert B., and Cynthia Fitterer Klingel. *Oceans.* Child's World, 2001.

Tocci, Salvatore. *Coral Reefs*. Franklin Watts, 2004.

Wroble, Lisa A. *The Oceans*. Endangered Animals & Habitats. Lucent Books, 1998.

Organizations and Online Sites

Oceanlink

http://oceanlink.island.net

This site contains many pages, including ones that have information on deep sea vents and an intertidal zone field guide, and offers visitors the opportunity to post a question to a marine scientist. You can also find interesting facts about marine animals, such as which fish is the fastest in the ocean and how big a blue whale can really get.

Pollution Solution

http://smithsonianeducation.org/educators/lesson_plans/ocean/pollution/essay.html

Find out how much oil enters the ocean each year from various sources. Learn what happens when people pour their used motor oil into the ground or septic system. This site also discusses how oil spills are cleaned up with the help of people and bacteria.

Exploring Estuaries

http://epa.gov/owow/estuaries/kids

Use this site to explore estuaries and learn more about some of the plants and animals that live in them. You can also solve a mystery and find out about the National Estuary Program, which is working to restore and protect these marine habitats.

What Is a Wetland?

http://wetland.org/educ_wetlandinfo2.htm

Find out how the soil differs in a swamp, a marsh, and a mangrove forest. You can also learn more about how plants are adapted to the high salt and low oxygen conditions in these marine habitats.

The Slime Filter

www.kawc.com/awpr/kyaw/kidseducation/ke2935.html

Learn how to make your own swamp water and how to filter it to remove the silt or sediment.

A Note on Sources

In checking my local library and online bookstores, I found several books with useful information on marine habitats. In fact, one book provided me with the idea of describing the *Trieste*'s dive into the Marianas Trench in the introduction. I followed up by checking the Internet for additional information about this world-record dive.

The Internet was my main source of information for most of this book. While reading through the materials I discovered, my main concern was in using only reliable sources. This meant focusing on reports, descriptions, summaries, and events provided by government agencies, environmental organizations, and marine research centers.

—*Salvatore Tocci*

Index

Numbers in *italics* indicate illustrations.

About the Author

Salvatore Tocci taught high school and college science for almost thirty years. He has a bachelor of arts degree from Cornell University and a master of philosophy degree from the City University of New York.

He has written books that deal with a range of science topics, from biographies about famous scientists to a high school chemistry textbook. He has also traveled throughout the United States to present workshops at national science conventions to show teachers how to emphasize to students the applications of scientific knowledge in everyday life.

Tocci lives in East Hampton, New York, with his wife, Patti. Both retired from teaching, they spend their leisure time during the warmer months sailing in coastal waters.